Tales from SYDNEY COVE

TALES FROM SYDNEY COVE

KATE CHALLIS

Edited by BERNARD SMITH

THE HELICON PRESS

First published in 2000 by
The Helicon Press Pty Ltd
21 Billyard Avenue / PO Box 918
Wahroonga NSW 2076
Telephone (02) 9487 8302
Facsimile (02) 9487 8303

The Author and Publisher gratefully acknowledge
financial assistance from the Sydney Harbour
Foreshore Authority and James Fairfax to enable
publication of this book.

National Library of Australia
Cataloguing-in-Publication data:

Challis, Kate.
Tales from Sydney Cove.
Bibliography.
Includes index.
ISBN 0 9586785 1 0.
1. Sydney (N.S.W.) – History – 1788-1851. 2. Sydney
Cove (N.S.W.). 3. Sydney Cove (N.S.W.) – Description
and travel. 4. Sydney Cove (N.S.W.) – Social
conditions. I. Smith, Bernard, 1916– . II. Title.
994.4102

Design and production by Alison Forbes
Colour separation by Colorific Pty Ltd, Melbourne
Printed in Hong Kong by South China Printing
Co. (1988) Ltd

CONTENTS

The first European ships to sail through Australian waters were Portuguese and Dutch. In 1770 Captain James Cook RN charted the east coast of the land then known as New Holland, claiming it for the British crown. In his journal he named the territory New South Wales.

Cook anchored first at Botany Bay, where his botanists discovered many exotic species of plants. It was Botany Bay that the British government chose as the site for a new penal settlement. With the loss of the American colonies, England's jails and prison-hulks were overflowing with convicts sentenced to transportation.

In 1787 a convoy of vessels under the command of Captain Arthur Phillip RN, governor designate, sailed for Botany Bay. They numbered two naval ships, Sirius and Supply, six convict transports and three store ships. These ships have become known as the First Fleet. Aboard were 1030 persons: 736 convicts and the rest naval personnel, marines and their families.

In January 1788 the First Fleet anchored at Botany Bay, which they soon discovered unsuitable for settlement. Sailing north through an opening Cook had called Port Jackson, Phillip discovered a

The First Fleet leaves England

magnificent natural harbour. A small cove on the southern shore, close to a freshwater stream, was chosen as the site of the new settlement. It was named Sydney Cove in honour of Lord Sydney, Secretary of State for Home Affairs and the Colonies.

Upon their arrival the Europeans found three indigenous tribes, or 'natives' as they called them, occupying the surrounding regions. The Dahrug occupied the coastal strip between Port Jackson and Botany Bay as far west as the Blue Mountains. To the north of Port Jackson were the Kurringgai and to the south were the Dharawal.

This account of relations between the settlers and the indigenous tribes is based upon the diaries of First Fleet members. It is illustrated with their drawings and watercolours. Tragically the Europeans were recording the native way of life at its point of dissolution. The smallpox they carried with them decimated Sydney's Aboriginal tribes so rapidly that within two years whole communities were reduced to a few disoriented survivors. Physical traces of their presence remain on the landscape, and memories are preserved in the oral tradition of descendants. The other major source of information about them is the First Fleet diaries and artworks that inspired this book.

These tales are true tales. They record incidents that took place during the very first years of settlement at Sydney Cove. These years were ones of continual struggle and hardship, both for Governor Phillip and for his officers. To the convicts in their charge there seemed little to hope for. First of all, a place for the settlement had to be carved out of the virgin bush, and huts built to house the people and the stores they had brought so far to keep them alive. Then regulations had to be framed to cope with the problems of everyday life, and friendly relations established with the natives, who viewed with fear and mistrust the arrival of these strangers in their land.

In the eighteenth century it was common practice to keep a diary of day-to-day events. Fortunately many of the naval officers who helped establish the colony of New South Wales did so. It is from the journals of Captain Hunter of the *Sirius*, Judge Collins, Lieutenants Watkin Tench, William Bradley and Ralph Clarke that these tales are largely drawn. Even the journal of James Boswell, perhaps the finest English diarist of the eighteenth century, has a place in this book.

The chapters on Arabanoo, Bennelong and Balooderry tell of the early attempts of the white men and the natives to live together, and of the troubles that arose.

Native life at Port Jackson in 1788 NATURAL HISTORY MUSEUM, LONDON

It was more than difficult for men of such different cultures to understand one another. Yet the attempt *was* made, and at times even affection seemed to grow up between them. Misunderstandings were not always tragic in outcome; sometimes they were highly amusing. 'Famine and Disaster' recounts the terrible hardships the colonists suffered when, weak from lack of food, they anxiously awaited a supply ship from England. Excursions were frequently made in search of fertile land for cultivation. 'An Excursion Inland' tells of one expedition which, though arduous, was enlivened by friendly encounters with the natives. Later chapters recount tales of heroism. In one Governor Phillip is wounded by a native spear at Manly in an attempt to maintain friendly relations with the native tribes. Another recounts the experiences of convict escapees, who chose to battle it out with the sea than to suffer a life of toil and starvation.

Perhaps these tales can help re-create for us the world of the first settlement at Sydney Cove, which is so different now from 1788. The old anchor of the *Sirius*, now in the National Maritime Museum, and the stone marking the site of the first Government House trace its past. These tales, recounting the courage and endurance of the colonists—both free and convict—and of the indigenous tribes, in their response to the European intruders, can help make them a living memory for us. They are the heritage of all Australians.

A portrait of Bennelong NATURAL HISTORY MUSEUM · LONDON

Native name Ben-nel-long

A. painted when angry after Botany Bay Colebee was

1 : CHARTING THE HARBOUR

On 26 January 1788 the last of the ships of the First Fleet sailed through the Heads of Port Jackson. Governor Phillip had found Botany Bay quite unsuitable for the new settlement. Captain Cook, however, had marked another harbour, which he called Port Jackson, on the map a few miles to the north. So Phillip set out with a small party to discover its potential. He found a harbour indeed! Here was a place where the entire British fleet could anchor in perfect safety in the roughest weather. Selecting a small cove for the settlement, he put back to Botany Bay to bring the fleet round. It was now more than eight months since they had sailed from Portsmouth.

Leaving Botany Bay, the fleet sailed the last few miles past a coast of wide beaches and white sandhills. Then, rounding the South Head, with the Pacific rollers behind them, they came up close to the two rugged headlands and at last found themselves in the harbour. It wound away before them with many sandy coves and rocky promontories.

All the officers were up on deck to see the new harbour that had so impressed Phillip. To Surgeon Bowes, aboard the *Lady Penrhyn*, the country on either side seemed grander than a nobleman's country seat in England. For here were grassy terraces, romantic grottoes and groves of tall and stately trees. The singing of the birds and the flight of the many parakeets, lorikeets and cockatoos gave an air of enchantment to the place. Yet how menacingly the huge rocks overhung the water, glistening in the summer sun. Truly, it was a strange place! Young Lieutenant Southwell, leaning on the rail, fancied he saw gorgeous palaces and the ruins of stately buildings among the trees on the fascinating islands they saw as they sailed upstream. How picturesque it all was, with the foreshores running away up the harbour far into the distance! What a picture it would make, he thought, with the natives brandishing their spears at the intruders amidst such romantic scenery!

The officers observed the tangled vegetation along the shores, and many wondered how rich the soil might be and how suitable for cultivating food for the new settlement. Yet all agreed that it was the finest harbour they had ever seen.

After running up in a westerly direction for four miles, they anchored in the small cove Governor Phillip had chosen for the settlement. He had called it Sydney Cove. What activity there was now, after the long months of waiting! Once on shore, the Governor erected the canvas house he had brought from England and gave orders to his officers and men. Convicts with axes cleared an area for the first tents, while others were busy unloading the necessary provisions. Aboard ship the other convicts waited impatiently to disembark.

On all sides of the new settlers the virgin bush stretched out unknown hundreds of miles; before them lay the blue waters of the harbour and their ships riding at anchor. These ships were their lifeline with the civilised world. Phillip knew that until roads and tracks had been cut through the bush, the new settlement would have to rely almost completely upon travel by water. At any rate, the harbour must be charted immediately. So two days after their arrival, he sent Captain Hunter of the *Sirius* to make a complete survey of Port Jackson. Hunter took with him one of his Lieutenants, William Bradley; Mr Keltie, Master of the *Sirius*; and a party of twelve seamen in two boats.

As they went about their work, they observed many natives on the shore running along the rocks after the boats. All appeared very friendly, and shouted invitations to land. At a point between Middle Head and Bradley's Point, the party decided to go ashore to take measurements. Seeing them in difficulty the natives indicated a safe landing place, for they were very curious to know more about these white people. What were they doing in their boats with their strange weapons? Were they men or women?

The entrance to Port Jackson from Grotto Point

...wth point in the entrance of Port Jackson.

A View in N.º S. Wales

The natives had never seen anything like it before. These new people seemed able to remove layers of their skin and take off the tops of their heads. It was a new experience for Captain Hunter and Lieutenant Bradley too, as they made mental notes for their journals. To Captain Hunter they were 'a straight, thin, well-made people, rather small in their limbs, but very active'. He observed the dark colour of their bodies, which were smeared with fat and crusted over with dust and sand. They had bushy beards and dark matted hair. Some had a hole bored through their nostrils, through which a bone was fastened as an ornament. Many of them had a front tooth missing. Governor Phillip was received with great approbation by the natives of Manly on his first visit to the harbour, when he showed them that he had a tooth missing in front too.

Today there is an obelisk to mark the spot where Phillip first landed in Port Jackson with his advance party, when looking for a place for the settlement. Here at Camp Cove, just inside the South Head, they lunched on the first day. As they cooked on the beach, friendly natives strolled up to watch. They came unarmed, leaving their spears on the sand some distance away, where their women were left in canoes for safety. The white man's method of boiling fish interested them very much; for themselves they just put their fish on the hot embers to warm. On one occasion, a man more curious than the rest put his hand into a billy of boiling water to examine the fish being cooked. How painful it was sometimes to understand the whiteman's ways!

After charting this area of the harbour, the party camped for the night at Grotto Point. As the natives were very interested in their movements, the Englishmen deemed it wiser to sleep on the longboat that night. They erected tents fore-and-aft for the purpose. Next morning they charted Middle Harbour, the natives running along the rocky plateau at the water's edge to meet them. They came unarmed again, carrying only their throwing sticks, while a man followed at some distance with a bundle of spears. He was the guard for the women, who were following behind the men. This behaviour pleased the party greatly; as Bradley wrote, 'It increased my favourable opinion in them very much'. It was the kind of thing an English gentleman would do. The party visited Castle Rock, noting the extent of the shallow water around it. Then, turning round, they passed Grotto Point and crossed The Sound—a piece of deep water—sailing to Spring Cove, just inside the North Head.

Governor Phillip had been here only the week before, and many of the natives were found wearing the presents he had brought them. These were the men whose manly appearance had prompted Phillip to call the place 'Manly'. There was great merriment when the party landed. The natives danced and sang, imitating the actions and speech of the white men, who returned the compliment. One of the natives had his hair combed by a seaman, which pleased him very much. The officers examined the native canoes. Bradley did not think much of them: 'They are far the worst canoes I ever saw or heard of', he wrote. They were indeed very simply made. A piece of bark was chosen of the length required, and both ends were then gathered up by lashing them with vines. To row the natives sat very erect upon the floor of the canoe using wooden paddles. If the canoe leaked, which was often the case, the man sitting nearest to the leak would bale the water out with a piece of wood, always remaining in an erect sitting position.

Later in the day, Hunter and his men took measurements in the upper part of the north arm of the harbour. Two native men joined them, examining the work being done with amazement, and strolled to the fire where the seamen were preparing a meal. Soon another man and an old woman appeared at the fire. The woman was old and ugly, and as Bradley pointed out: 'We could not judge from her what the younger ones might be'. It seemed that the young women were not risking such an interview, though they could be seen spying through the branches some distance away. Signs were made to invite them to the fire. The officers explained, as best they could, that they would give the presents the natives were clamouring for to those women who would come for them.

Dinner was then eaten in privacy on the longboat. By this time, as many as eighty natives had assembled on the beach. And then, as the white men dined at a safe distance from the shore, the women came slowly out from the shelter of the trees. They were accompanied by an armed guard who had ornamented their bodies

A Native going to Fish with a Torch and Flambeaux while his Wife and children are broiling fish for their Supper with white and red clay. The men had drawn white circles around their eyes, a horizontal line across their foreheads and broad white lines down their limbs. They look like so many skeletons, thought Captain Hunter, as he saw them coming down to the beach. In their hands they carried green boughs as a sign of peace, and drew themselves up in a line behind the women. Two armed scouts were also posted on a headland overlooking the boats.

The officers made signs that they would bring the presents to the women via the small boat. But as they rowed to the shore, the women ran for shelter to the trees. The officers in their turn put back towards the longboat. These overtures might have gone on indefinitely had not an old man, who seemed to be a leader of the tribe, taken things into his own hands. He directed the women to come down to the water's edge. Instantly the guards were all attention, their spears poised ready to throw as the old man received the officers. It was his intention to hand the presents over to the women, but the officers would have none of that. The women must come themselves.

Finally one of the young women summoned up enough courage to come quite close. She seemed afraid but managed to laugh as they ornamented her with beads and buttons, which pleased her very much. The others then followed her, laughing and trembling, to get their gifts. The old man led forward the more timid, who stretched out their arms for presents, standing as far away as they possibly could.

How Bradley admired, as he said, the appearance of these young women with their straight bodies, good features and musical voices. Only two could not be coaxed to come. When all the women had presented themselves, the officers rowed away triumphantly. Now the armed guard on the shore could relax. And immediately they put down their spears and began dancing and singing.

Maps of the Lane Cove and the Parramatta Rivers still had to be made. The natives in these upper reaches of the harbour were found to be very fearful and hostile. The settlers supposed that these natives had fled from the settlement to safer places. One party along the Parramatta River, seeing the boats approaching, left their fire where they were cooking mussels, and ran for their lives. The officers landing found their canoes on the beach and the weapons they had left nearby. Taking great care that nothing should be disturbed, they left gifts around the fire and in the canoes, hoping in this way to gain the natives' confidence and friendship. This proved the case, for the next day, while cooking breakfast at a place afterwards called Breakfast Point, the frightened natives of the day before came up in their canoes. The Englishmen straight away invited them over, showing their friendly disposition by waving green boughs. Soon seven men joined them and seated themselves about the fire. They would not sample the whitemen's breakfast, but were interested in all that was going on. They had brought along their own breakfast of mussels to prepare and cook on the fire which the officers were good enough to leave for their use.

Beyond Breakfast Point the land became flat, with mangrove swamps along the shores. Narrow channels opened out on all sides, up which the frightened natives disappeared in their canoes. Captain Hunter, seeing the harbour was no longer navigable for shipping, decided to put back to Sydney Cove. The party brought back maps of Port Jackson with the soundings, plotting the rocks and shoals and indicating safe channels for their ships. During the survey they had seen many fish and warned the settlers that the harbour was full of sharks. They had also found supplies of food growing locally. Oysters could be found in the coves with muddy bottoms, with other edible shellfish. The wild spinach, samphire and other leaves they had used, so they said, could supply the settlement with green vegetables. The party had at all times been careful, as we have seen, to observe the Governor's instructions to win the friendship and confidence of the natives. Altogether they had been out ten days and had finished their survey 'in as accurate a manner as time allowed'.

2 : ARABANOO

*I*t was no easy matter for the white men and the natives to live peaceably side by side. A state of fear and uneasiness soon developed. A white man straying from the settlement in search of leaves for making tea went in fear of native spears; perhaps he had taken some native fish-hooks from the rocks. A native making a close inspection of the white man's garden plot would be chased off unceremoniously and forced to return the shovel or axe he might have taken. These suspicions and fears often gave rise to unnecessary acts of violence, which only heightened the tension between the white and black inhabitants of Port Jackson.

In December 1788 the natives attacked the convicts employed making bricks. A terrified messenger reported to the Governor that two thousand natives were assembled. A detachment of soldiers was then sent to them at Brickfield Hill, where they soon found the report was greatly exaggerated. The fact of the matter was that

about fifty natives had advanced menacingly, but were scared off when the convicts pointed their spades and shovels at them pretending to be about to shoot.

It was incidents such as these which greatly worried Governor Phillip. He believed that if some natives were captured a friendly understanding could be reached. He hoped that the natives would learn to speak English, and by kind treatment become friendly interpreters for him among their own people.

For this purpose, Lieutenants Ball and Johnstone were sent down the harbour in two boats to seize some men. At Manly they saw a group of natives on the beach. Rowing close to the shore they offered them beads and other trinkets. The natives approached the boats, and when two were close enough, ropes were thrown over their heads. In the struggle which followed one native escaped. The other unfortunate was dragged into the boat. He screamed with fear expecting to be murdered on the spot. His wild cries for help brought back the others who had fled to the bush. They attacked the boat with spears, stones and firebrands. So the boat was quickly rowed out of range, and at a safe distance from the shore, the rope was removed from the terrified prisoner's neck and tied to one of his legs. The two officers comforted him and encouraged him to eat some fish.

Their mission accomplished they put back to the Cove. When they arrived at Sydney there was quite a stir. Until now natives had only been casual visitors at the settlement. But here was one who would have to stay by government order. About thirty years of age, strongly built, he was quite good-looking for a native, the settlers thought. Many came down to the wharf to see him, and even the upstairs windows of Government House were filled with curious onlookers. But the poor man was very upset by it all. Yet there was plenty to interest him. Those people waving to him with their heads sticking out of the upstairs windows of Government House quite amazed him. He pointed to them excitedly. And though the dogs frightened him at first, he was quite taken with cats and the chickens pecking about the grounds!

At Government House Phillip welcomed him and invited him to dine at his own side-table. He ate his fish and duck with relish, when cooled, but smelt the bread, salt-meat and wine suspiciously. Of course he ate with his fingers, and finding no better place cleaned his hands on his chair. So they gave him a towel, which he used 'with great cleanliness and decency'.

Then, when he had dined, the officers thought he should be cleaned. First his hair, matted with dirt, was cut and combed. It was alive with vermin too, and to the great horror of the watching officers, he swallowed them as they fell from his head. Apparently he preferred them to bread and wine. But seeing their looks of disapproval he desisted. Next they decided to shave him, but he was terrified by the sight of the razor and would not consent until he had seen one of the convicts shaved first. Finally a tub of hot, soapy water was brought and he was scrubbed from head to foot. The officers, who were not yet certain of the colour of the natives (their bodies being so coated with grease, dirt and dust), noted that his skin was quite a light brown colour. Being clean, he was then clothed in a shirt, jacket and trousers. The white men did not want their native to escape, so they made him wear leg-irons. How pleased he was with them—after all they were quite the vogue in Sydney! The officers jokingly told him they were *bang-ally*, a native word meaning decorations. But later he learned the real reason for these whiteman's bangles and was very angry to have been deceived.

The young man would not tell them his name, for among his people names were only exchanged with friends. So they called him Manly, after the place where they had captured him. Washed, shaved and dressed, Manly was shown some picture-books. Among them was a book of animal pictures. The Governor hoped by this means to establish the existence of Australian animals still unknown to the new settlers. But he met with no success, since Manly was also curious about animals he had not seen. It was the elephants and rhinoceros which interested him. Yet he wanted to please. They had managed to teach him that a female convict was called a woman, so 'woman' he exclaimed happily, pointing to a portrait of the elegant Duchess of Cumberland, to the amusement and delight of all present.

Phillip had already prepared a hut in the grounds of Government House to accommodate the captured natives, and to it Manly was brought in the evening. A trustworthy convict was given charge of him, leading him by a rope attached to his leg-irons and sleeping in the hut with him at night. Here Manly was allowed to cook his own supper. The method was simple; first he threw the fish on an open fire just as it was. When it was warm, he took it off, rubbed off the scales and peeled it with his teeth, eating the skin. Then he cleaned and threw it on the fire again to warm.

The next morning the officers found Manly sullen and miserable. So they took him round the settlement to see the sights. From the Observatory at Dawes Point, he could see the smoke of native fires across the harbour. He sighed deeply and said '*gwee-un*', (meaning 'fire'). His appetite at breakfast was not, however, affected by his melancholy mood, for he ate eight fish, each weighing about a pound. Later, as he sat musing with his back to the fire, his shirt caught alight. After that shock the officers had great difficulty in persuading him to put on another to meet the Governor. For that very day was 1 January 1789.

The officers celebrated New Year's Day by dining at Government House. And there at the Governor's high table, near the window, was Manly seated on a chest, wearing his second shirt. He ate roast pork and fish, using his towel with great refinement. But finding no use for his empty plate, he would have thrown it through the open window had not those nearby prevented him. After the tables were cleared, singing and music began. Phillip hoped that Manly would enjoy the music, for he had a soft, musical voice and was known to imitate the tunes he heard. But the music had no charms for him; besides he had just eaten a large meal and felt very drowsy. So, putting his hat under his head as a pillow, he stretched himself out on his chest and went to sleep. It was most disappointing.

It was part of Phillip's plan that the natives should see Manly well and happy. In the hope that he would tell his friends about the kindness he had received, Phillip had him taken to Manly by boat. The natives came down to talk with him. Although no one in the boat could follow the conversation, it seemed that they were asking him why he did not run away, for he was seen pointing to his leg-irons. Manly was very dejected, and wept as he spoke to them. Yet he was quite willing to return to Sydney, where he cooked two kangaroo rats and not less than three pounds of fish for his supper, we are told.

Then, one day in February, the *Supply* set sail for Norfolk Island. Phillip accompanied the ship down the harbour, taking Manly with him. But the outing was no fun to the young native, who was terrified. He had been made a prisoner on a boat once before by the whitemen, and this time it seemed they were taking him far from his country. Watching his chance, he suddenly leapt to the rail and plunged overboard. Rising to the surface he struck out for the shore. As he expected them to fire at him from the ship, he attempted to submerge himself and swim underwater; but though Manly was known to be an expert swimmer and diver, the buoyancy of his clothes, an eyewitness said, prevented him. Quickly a boat was lowered and Manly was picked up struggling. How silent and melancholy he was; he had given up hope of ever returning home. Then imagine his happiness, when the Governor called to him, and they both descended into a boat! He sprang forward, cheerful and confident again, as he realised that he was returning. For the rest of the day, we are told, he was excessively happy.

In the end he began to like Sydney. The leg-irons were now no longer necessary, as he was quite happy to stay. Even his own countrymen showed little interest in him the next time he was taken to visit, though he talked to them in a friendly manner, offering presents. He soon learned the officers' names, and in his turn told them his own, which was Arabanoo. He showed great courtesy to the ladies. The children liked him; he would fondle them and offer them tit-bits from his plate when he was dining. Even the dogs and cats followed him about. In fact everybody liked him, and he was beginning to enjoy himself. He had grown to enjoy the whiteman's food, especially the bread and the tea. Captain Hunter, on returning to Sydney after a voyage to the Cape, was surprised to find Arabanoo drinking tea with the Governor and his friends: 'He managed his cup and saucer as well, as though he had been long accustomed to such entertainment'. Hunter found him so good-natured and so easy to talk to that he invited him to dine on board his ship, the *Sirius*, with the Governor.

Arabanoo learned English slowly. He enjoyed the time after dinner when he was teacher to the officers, instructing them in his native language. He would make them say each word over distinctly and laugh at their attempts. At last it seemed that Phillip's experiment was bearing fruit.

But in April people began to wonder why there were so few natives on the shores of the harbour. Later many were found dead or dying of smallpox in the caves along the foreshores. Among the natives a sick person was left to die alone; he was not even supplied with food to eat. Some sick natives were brought to Sydney for treatment; others, getting no help from their own people, began to come to the hospital. Arabanoo took it upon himself to nurse many of them, but in spite of his kindness and devotion, in nearly all cases the sickness proved fatal. A young boy, Nanberee, survived and was adopted by the Surgeon, Mr White, and a girl also, who was taken into the home of the Rev. Richard Johnson. Both these children grew up happily in their new homes, but knew very little about their own people.

In May it became apparent that Arabanoo himself was developing smallpox. Though medicines were given to him, and every care taken, he died after six days. The Governor was sad to lose him. He had him buried in his own garden and personally attended the funeral. Arabanoo had proved a good-natured, lovable companion and a faithful friend. He was keen to learn and always ready to talk about the ways and customs of his own people. With Arabanoo Phillip had made his first attempt to establish peaceful relations between the settlers and the natives. If it had not been a success, it pointed to what might still be done.

A portrait of Nanberee <small>NATURAL HISTORY MUSEUM, LONDON</small>

NANBERRY, a Native
BOY of PORT JACKSON, living
with Mr White — the Surg. Gen.

3 : FAMINE AND DISASTER

*A*lthough the guests at the Governor's table enjoyed a very fine turtle from Lord Howe Island to celebrate Christmas 1789, the new year which followed was to be no time of celebration in the young settlement. For with it came the threat of famine, a threat increased by the loss of the Sirius.

Indeed the settlement felt deserted by its homeland. It was dependent on England for its food supply, but for two long years not one new ship had sailed through the heads of Port Jackson. Yet the long vigil for a sail never ceased; should a gun boom without warning, or a clap of thunder resound from the sea, there was a stir of expectancy. Was it a ship at last? The whole settlement felt as though it were shipwrecked on a barren land and forgotten. All their hopes were turned towards the sea. Parties went every week to Botany Bay to see whether a ship had arrived there, since this was the place originally chosen by the British Government for the settlement. A lookout post was erected on the South Head, where a watch was stationed and a flag could be hoisted to announce the arrival of a ship to the people at Sydney Cove.

The food position had become perilous. The provisions were getting very short and were deteriorating. Great rats were ravaging the stores, and much food had become rotten through the heavy rains. The pork had been salted for over three years, and the very grains of rice were teeming with vermin. So old and dry was the pork that it would shrink to half its size when boiled. So it was cut into small pieces instead, and toasted on a fork in front of a fire. The drops of fat falling from it were caught on the slices of bread or in saucers of rice. The flour that remained, however, was good. For Captain Hunter had recently been sent to the Cape to purchase some to supplement the provisions. Lieutenant Tench, who endured these hardships and has described them better than anyone else, tells us how the soldiers and convicts boiled up the flour with their greens to make the meal go further. Efforts at raising crops and growing vegetables had not been very successful. Even the fish were not as abundant in the early months of the year.

The food situation being so acute, Phillip decided to send two shiploads of convicts to Norfolk Island. Here the soil had proved more productive, and consequently the smaller settlement had made somewhat better progress than the parent settlement in Sydney. The *Supply* and the *Sirius* sailed on 6 March 1790 under

Lieutenant-Governor Ross, with a couple of marines and convicts, taking a supply of provisions with them.

Lieutenant Southwell, posted at the South Head lookout, has told us how he watched them sail through the Heads and out to sea, and how he wondered how many days it would be before he sighted another vessel. It happened sooner than he had expected. For a few weeks later, at dawn on 5 April, a sail hove into sight. It was not long before Southwell recognised the *Supply* returning. What did this mean? Had the *Sirius* been wrecked? And were the decks crowded with people? He notified Phillip immediately. The Governor decided to go down the harbour to meet the vessel. Lieutenant Tench, who was in the boat with Phillip, tells us how on rounding one of the points of the harbour, a boat from the *Supply* came into view. In it was Lieutenant Ball, who was making signs to indicate that some accident had happened. Coming alongside he was able to relate in full the disaster which had occurred.

It appears that when the *Sirius* reached Norfolk Island there was strong surf running in Sydney Bay, where the settlement had been established. It was not safe to make a landing there. But at Cascade Bay a landing was found possible, though only in one place, where a rock projected some distance into deep water. All the marines and convicts were successfully landed. But the sky was becoming overcast. A strong wind blew up, and drove the ship not only from the bay, but out of sight

A native woman presenting her man with a fish NATURAL HISTORY MUSEUM, LONDON

of land. So the *Sirius* returned to Sydney Bay, where they found a high surf still running. A signal from the shore, however, told them that boats could be landed with safety on the beach. So longboats were lowered and sent ashore with provisions, while the *Sirius* rolled in the surf.

The *Supply*, which had also been driven from the island, was now in the bay unloading. From its deck, Lieutenant Ball waved his hat frantically to Hunter on the *Sirius*. Hunter, alarmed, saw him pointing to a dangerous reef of sunken rocks lying off the west point of the bay. In the confusion of unloading in a heavy sea, no one on the *Sirius* had noticed that the vessel was steadily drifting towards the reef. Captain Hunter immediately took steps to prevent her drifting further. He tried to tack this way and that to escape the danger, but the wind prevented him. The anchor tore away, and the ship struck the reef. Immediately water flowed into the holds. Hunter ordered the masts to be cut, but she was soon a complete wreck. Fortunately the *Sirius* was wrecked stern foremost with her bows to sea; broadside on she would have been overturned. All hands were ordered to bring the provisions up onto the gun deck, as already the water in the hold was seven feet deep. In the evening the wind grew stronger, and Captain Hunter was warned by signals from the shore to quit the ship.

Lieutenant Bradley, who was on board the *Sirius* with Captain Hunter, has described how the remainder of the ship's company was brought to safety. He tells how they managed to get a hawser from the ship to the land by throwing a cask overboard to which a small rope was attached. This was driven by the surf to shore. By this means those on shore were able to pull in the heavy hawser, attached to the ship's end of the rope. The hawser they made fast to a pine tree. A piece of wood with a hole in it was threaded through the hawser, to which a grating was attached like a pair of scales. Two lines were fastened to either side of the wood; one for hauling to the shore, the other for hauling the empty traveller back to the ship. On this precarious contrivance the ship's company was successfully brought to shore through the heavy surf. They travelled two or more at a time on the grating, the surf continuously breaking over them, so that many arrived bruised, senseless and half-drowned. Captain Hunter himself was badly bruised and buffeted when landing. It was even feared that he might lose hold of the grating.

Fortunately, a few days later the weather improved sufficiently for unloading the provisions. Some strong swimmers among the seamen swam to the wreck, and many casks of provisions were hauled ashore on the traveller, about twenty to thirty a day. Some, however, were washed off the traveller and dashed against the rocks. There now being 506 people on the island on half-allowance of rations, every effort was made to bring the provisions to shore, as the ship was expected to break up at any time. In their zeal some things were thrown over the ship's side to float to shore, but many heavy packages among them sank to the bottom and were lost. In this way the officers lost many of their possessions, all of the contents of the cabins being thrown overboard. To prevent theft a guard was stationed along the beach to collect anything that came washed ashore.

Later two convicts were allowed to help salvage the ship. They swam to the *Sirius* to throw the livestock overboard. First they threw the pigs over, then the goats. Then they found the liquor, but they did not throw that overboard. Instead they sat on the gun deck and got thoroughly drunk. And in this condition, somehow or other they set the ship on fire. A third convict volunteered to put it out. He swam to the ship, got the other two off, and after putting out the fire remained all night as a safeguard.

When most of the provisions had been unloaded, strong seas blew up again. The cable holding the ship's head was severed by the rocks, and the ship was lifted round and driven nearer to shore by about a length. This brought the *Sirius* into calmer water where it was easier to board her. Unloading was now, however, a dangerous business. The beams of the ship were loosened or broken by the sea, and all the decks moved with the tide, so the holds could not be safely entered to get out supplies. Sometime afterwards the guns and gun carriages were brought ashore on a traveller. Many years later they landed the anchor of the *Sirius*, which may now be seen at the National Maritime Museum, Darling Harbour.

Lieutenant Ball was not able to tell Phillip the whole story of the wreck, as the *Supply* had sailed for Port Jackson before a start had been made in landing the

The wreck of the Sirius NATURAL HISTORY MUSEUM, LONDON

provisions. It was therefore assumed that the need for food at Norfolk Island was greater than it actually was. The Governor called a conference immediately to consider the food situation. First they calculated how long the existing supply of food would last on the present ration. It was found that the salt meat would last until 2 July, and the flour until 20 August. Rice and peas could then be used as a substitute for flour until 1 October. Because of the seriousness of the situation, it was agreed that the rations should be reduced still further. They were now to be two pounds of pork, two and a half pounds of flour, and two pounds of rice or a quarter of a pound of peas per person for a week.

So meagre a diet demanded that a special effort be made to gather more food locally. Everyone was expected to contribute. Fishing parties were organised in which all helped, even the Rev. Richard Johnson, who was a bad sailor. (His lack of enthusiasm is obvious from his letters home.) The best shots were sent out after game; kangaroos were especially sought after. Because people were weak from lack of food, working hours had to be reduced. This also gave more time for gathering food. Phillip finally decided to send the *Supply* to Batavia to purchase supplies. For still no one knew when a ship would arrive from England.

Three more months dragged by. Then one day in June Lieutenant Tench, coming out of his hut, heard the cry 'The flag is up!' and was surprised to see women kissing their children in the streets and everyone weeping for joy. He tells us how excitedly he ran up a hill with one of his brother officers to see the new ship making its way up the harbour: 'We could not speak; we wrung each other by the hand, with eyes and hearts overflowing'. It was the *Lady Juliana* transport, the first ship of the Second Fleet. It was their first contact with England for three long years. Up the harbour went the Governor to meet her. How pleased they were to read at last the large letters 'LONDON' on her stern. They urged one another to row faster: 'Pull away, my lads! She's from Old England! A few more strokes and we shall be aboard! Hurrah for a bellyful and news from our friends!'. After the greetings came the newspapers, and the letters. 'News broke upon us like meridian splendour on a blind man', exclaims Tench in his journal. And what news it was! A revolution had broken out in France that was to change the history of the world, while in England George III had gone mad but was now sane again.

The local news was less exciting. In the next few days the transports full of sick, starved and wretched convicts arrived. England had indeed not forgotten the infant colony. Here were another thousand convicts, most of them quite unfit for the heavy work needed to set the colony upon its feet.

*W*e have heard in the story of Arabanoo, despite its unfortunate ending, that Governor Phillip was doing his best to create friendly relations between the natives and the colonists. By going among them unarmed, offering gifts and treating them with courtesy and kindness, he had gained their confidence. Natives began to visit the settlement bringing their wives and babies. The soldiers amused themselves giving bread to the little dark children, who soon learnt to say 'hungry' and 'bread', showing how hungry they were by drawing in their tummies appealingly. But the native visitors, being suspicious, did not stay overnight. Nor is this surprising when we remember how Arabanoo was captured and forced to remain at Sydney Cove. Indeed although Phillip's intentions were good, his methods to our eyes are certainly open to question.

Following the death of Arabanoo, two other young natives, Bennelong and Colbee, were seized. Lieutenant Bradley was ordered to capture the two men. Meet-

Two boys practising spear throwing NATURAL HISTORY MUSEUM, LONDON

Two Native Boys of New south Wales — practising throwing the Spear this they do with small twigs cut on purpose

A View in Port Jackson 1792.

———————

ing the settlement's fishing boat as he rowed up the harbour, he got some fish to entice the natives. On reaching Manly he saw some men hauling their canoes on shore. He called to them, holding up the fish, and two more friendly than the rest left their companions and approached the boat. They had left their spears on the rocks and talked happily to the crew now on shore, while four others remained at the oars ready to row away. Then, as the two natives were dancing together, Lieutenant Bradley gave the signal. The men Bennelong and Colbee were seized, and thrown struggling into the boat to be lashed to the thwarts. Immediately the boat was pulled out from the shore, leaving a scene of great distress. The men cried furiously after the boat, while the women and children screamed with fear. The captives were terrified, though one called angrily to his friends on shore for help. 'It was by far the most unpleasant service I ever was ordered to execute', writes Lieutenant Bradley with some feeling in his journal.

On arrival the men were carefully guarded, and led by ropes attached to their leg-irons. Yet while appearing contented, they were always watching for a chance to escape. Colbee managed to get away seventeen days later. Sitting at supper in the natives' hut, the convicts in charge were busily employed eating while Colbee sat on the doorstep with his back to his keepers. He found that he was able to detach the rope from his leg-irons. Quick as a flash he was over the wooden paling to freedom, leg-irons and all. Bennelong, on the other hand, stayed six months. He made his

The taking of Colbee

escape by night. Pretending to be feeling ill, he asked to go upstairs, but eluding his keeper he too leapt the fence and got safely away.

Some months later, in September 1790, Governor Phillip rowed up the harbour to make arrangements for the erection of a column on the South Head to mark the entrance to the harbour. With him were two of his officers, Mr Collins the Judge Advocate and Lieutenant Waterhouse. Their task completed, they were rowing back to Sydney Cove when they met another party returning from Manly. The others said they had seen Bennelong and Colbee, who had given them a present of whale-meat for the Governor. Bennelong and Colbee wanted Phillip to visit them at Manly, where the whale had been stranded. They said that they would visit him at Government House, if he would come to see them. Phillip decided to go, and put back to the South Head to collect four muskets and a pistol for protection, together with some gifts for the natives. He then rowed across the Heads to Manly.

Approaching the beach they saw a large group of natives gathered on the sand. They were clustering round a fire cooking whale-meat, while the dead whale, somewhat putrefied and causing an unpleasant smell, was lying in the water some yards from the shore. Governor Phillip went ashore alone and unarmed, holding his arms out in a manner made famous by Captain Cook, leaving his officers and men with muskets ready in case of accident. But Bennelong and Colbee were nowhere to be seen. So Phillip called out in native language: 'I am the Governor, your father', which was the way Bennelong had addressed him at Government House. Then, sure enough, came Bennelong's answer from the bush nearby, 'Here I am', and they met under the trees and shook hands.

Returning to the boat Phillip brought ashore food and presents: wine, beef, bread, knives and jackets. The natives were delighted, but for the moment Bennelong and Colbee were nowhere to be seen. Again Phillip returned to the boat, and brought back Collins with him. They found Bennelong and Colbee had returned. Bennelong had donned two jackets, but Colbee could not manage his and had to get Lieutenant Waterhouse, who by this time had already joined them, to help him. They opened a bottle of wine, and drinking together talked of the good times they had passed at Government House. Bennelong enquired after his friend the French cook, mimicking his mannerisms as he used to do at Government House, to the great amusement of the officers. He asked after the health of a lady he had once kissed. And recollecting the happy moment, he kissed Lieutenant Waterhouse and laughed heartily. The Governor admired the beautiful long spear Bennelong had with him. How he would have liked it for a gift! But Bennelong refused to part with it, and laying it on the ground at his feet for safety, gave Phillip a throwing stick instead.

So they talked, and the natives began to gather round interested in what was going on. Gradually quite a crowd of them collected, forming a semicircle about the party. Each native was armed with a spear. The Governor, sensing possible danger, felt it wise to return to the boat while there was still a way open. For the semicircle was fast becoming a circle of armed natives. He told Bennelong that he would visit him again in two days, bringing more presents, including a hatchet, which Bennelong frequently asked for, and the clothes he had worn at Government House. Bennelong seemed pleased at this. But he wished to introduce the Governor to a few of his friends before Phillip left. There was Willemering, for instance. The Governor, thinking him an important member of the tribe, went to him holding out his hand, meaning to shake him by the hand. But Willemering, it seems, became very alarmed. Perhaps he recalled the fate of Arabanoo, and the capture of his friends Bennelong and Colbee. At any rate, fearing that he was going to be taken prisoner, he rushed forward, picked up Bennelong's beautiful spear, and quick as a flash fixed it to a throwing stick. Phillip, seeing his danger, shouted 'Wee-ree, wee-ree', meaning 'Bad, you are doing wrong'. But this had no effect. The spear struck him under the collarbone, piercing him through the right shoulder.

Then everyone became excited. Collins hurried to the boat to get the muskets, while Lieutenant Waterhouse helped Phillip to the boat as best he could. Spears now flew about them on all sides, coming from every direction. Phillip did his best to hold up the spear with both hands, but the shaft being so long struck the ground as he ran. This caused him severe pain and made his wound bleed freely, besides

Lt Waterhouse trying to break the spear impaling Governor Phillip's shoulder Natural History Museum, London

Mr Waterhouse endeavouring to break the Spear after Govr Phillips was wounded by We-it-me-wing) where the Whale was cast on Shore in Manly Cove.

hindering his progress to the boat. Realising this, he cried: 'Haul it out, Water-house, for God's sake'. Waterhouse did his best, but the spear was barbed and too deeply embedded to draw out. So he tried to break the shaft by jerking it this way and that. Just when he was thinking that he would never be able to break it, a spear thrown with great accuracy took the skin off his thumb and forefinger. Stung by the pain, Lieutenant Waterhouse found the added strength he needed to snap the spear. Meanwhile the marines had formed a line between them and the natives. They fired the two muskets, and Phillip, now freed from the weight of the spear shaft and enraged by the turn of events, stopped and fired a few shots from his pistol into the bush.

The attack repulsed, Governor Phillip was lifted into the boat almost fainting from loss of blood. The sailors, fearing that the wound might prove fatal, rowed so well that they covered the five miles to Sydney Cove within two hours. There Mr Balmain, the Surgeon, soon extracted the spearhead and dressed the wound, saying that there was no cause for alarm. Indeed in six weeks the Governor was completely recovered.

Bennelong seemed to be truly sorry that the accident had happened. A few days later he came to a cove near the settlement with his wife and companions, and asked to speak with the officers. He wanted the Governor to understand that both he and Colbee had beaten Willemering severely, though it had been fear which made him act so foolishly. Bennelong then camped near the settlement for ten days, hoping to see the Governor. On the tenth day Phillip was well enough to see him and accept his apology.

On the day before, some convicts had pulled in two great hauls of fish, about four thousand, each weighing nearly five pounds. They called them salmon because they resembled somewhat the salmon they had caught at home in England. Governor Phillip had thirty to forty taken to Bennelong as a token of their enduring friendship. After this Bennelong was seen frequently at Government House. The Governor even built a hut for him at his request, on the east side of Sydney Cove, at the place still called Bennelong Point today

5 : MORE ABOUT BENNELONG

Friendly relations continued between Phillip and Bennelong, though at first he was suspicious about visiting Government House, fearing he might be forced to stay. A friendly meeting with some officers on the north shore gave him confidence and ended in his visiting Government House again.

At this meeting the officers and Bennelong had a picnic of wine, bread and beef. Bennelong had acquired a taste for wine. After the meal, Bennelong was shaved at his request, and his friends who were watching allowed their beards to be clipped with scissors. Bennelong wanted Barangaroo, his wife, to have her hair cut too. For the occasion she put on a petticoat, but soon took it off when everyone laughed at her. Contests of bodily strength followed; one of the seamen lifted two of the natives from the ground with ease and was acclaimed by all present. A few days after this gaiety, the party met again, and a visit to Government House was

A view of Governor Phillip's house at Sydney Cove NATURAL HISTORY MUSEUM, LONDON

A View of Governor Philip's House Sydney Cove Port Jackson taken from the N.N.W.

proposed. Bennelong seemed quite agreeable, but Barangaroo refused absolutely and was very angry to see Bennelong preparing to go. She kicked and screamed and tore her hair, and threw Bennelong's best fishing spear on the ground with such violence that it broke. But Bennelong did not notice the scene she was making, being more interested in getting into the boat for Sydney Cove with some of his native friends. The Rev. Richard Johnson, who was left as a hostage to reassure Bennelong that he would be brought safely home, was left to manage Barangaroo. Her husband gone, she became calm and settled down by the fire to make fish-hooks.

Bennelong and his friends had a most enjoyable time on arriving at the settlement. At Government House they received various presents, among them some hatchets, which they always prized highly. Bennelong soon felt at home again. It was the first time he had been inside Government House since his escape. He ran from room to room, introducing the natives to his old friends in a most familiar way, and kissed the Governor's orderly affectionately. We are told how he tried to explain the use of a snuffer to his companions, saying 'nuffer' and 'candle', while holding up a finger as a candle, pretending to snuff it; but they could not understand what he meant. Angry at their lack of understanding, he soon showed them something else. Bennelong was pleased to see the Governor, and in taking his leave expressed a desire to visit him again. The Governor took care that the natives should be allowed to go as soon as they asked. On returning to Bennelong's camp, they found Barangaroo still making fish-hooks by the fire with the Rev. Richard Johnson sitting beside her. She was still angry with Bennelong and pretended not to notice him. But he noticed her, and the fish spear too that she had broken in her bad temper before he left. It was his turn to be very angry. She would have got a bad beating on the back of the head, the usual way in which the natives punished their wives, had not the officers interfered. Her sullenness disappeared, however, at the sight of the new petticoat Bennelong had brought her. She put it on and behaved in a very lofty manner, which curiously enough put him into a good temper again.

Bennelong began to feel a man of consequence Shortly after the visit to Government House, Phillip had built him a brick hut, twelve foot square. He dined at Government House frequently, wearing his red coat with silver epaulettes and nankeen breeches, his Sunday clothes. On other occasions he wore a jacket of the coarsest red jersey and a pair of trousers. Phillip gave him these thick clothes intentionally, hoping that he would feel cold without them and so always go about clothed. But the plan was not successful. On some days Bennelong would be walking about in his clothes, but on other days he would saunter about the settlement quite naked, with his clothes bundled into a net which he tied around his neck. Barangaroo was pleased with the hut too. She felt very well dressed when she walked out with a small bone ornamenting her nose. On rare occasions, perhaps as a gesture to the conventions of the Englishmen, she wore a petticoat.

Bennelong's hut became a meeting place for the natives visiting Sydney. Sometimes there were friendly gatherings; on other occasions fierce quarrels took place there.

One day many natives were seen about the hut calling 'Bennelong' and '*Dee-in*', which meant 'woman'. The Governor, writing at his desk, was interrupted by Bennelong, who appeared to be in a bad humour. He announced that he was going to beat a woman with a hatchet, and kill her in his hut. The Governor, concerned by Bennelong's wild appearance and dangerous behaviour, decided to accompany him back to the hut, taking Judge Collins and an orderly sergeant with him. On the way, Collins tried to explain the legal position to Bennelong, pointing out that if he killed the girl the Governor would have to kill him. This apparently meant nothing to Bennelong, for in reply to Collins he drew his finger across his head, arms and chest, to show where he intended to wound the girl before finally dispatching her with his hatchet. At this Phillip insisted upon taking away Bennelong's hatchet, which he had made very sharp.

On arrival at the hut they found a few natives lounging around the fire and the poor girl cowering in the corner. She was only sixteen, the daughter of the Chief of the Cameragal tribe, which Bennelong hated. They were old enemies and

Bennelong had often sought to enlist the Governor's aid to fight them. Bennelong had seized the girl at Broken Bay, meaning to avenge himself upon his enemy. On entering the hut, Bennelong immediately seized a wooden sword and hit the girl on the head twice, wounding her. Then, becoming very excited, he brandished his spear at the Governor, and shouted for his hatchet. Fortunately the *Supply* was just offshore. A longboat with muskets was soon landed, and Bennelong restrained by force. The girl, now unconscious, was taken to the hospital, together with a young man who said that he was her husband. Bennelong, still undeterred, sent a party of his friends, led by Bigon, to the hospital to carry them both off, but they were soon sent away.

Then, a few days later, Bennelong visited the girl himself. His attitude towards her had apparently changed. Indeed he spoke so kindly to her that his wife Barangaroo became jealous, and threw stones at the poor girl, and tried to beat her over the head with a club.

Yet Bennelong did not always have it all his own way in the frequent brawls at his hut. After one of them, he and Barangaroo were allowed to sleep in one of the back bedrooms of Government House at their request. Apparently the hut was not safe enough that night. They asked Phillip to lock them in, and to kindly keep the key in his pocket.

It was about this time that Barangaroo went to the Governor to tell him that she was about to have a child. She said that she 'intended doing him the honour', as Captain Hunter puts it, of having her baby at Government House. But Phillip managed to persuade her that the hospital would suit her better. Much interest was aroused as to the preparations she would make for her new baby. But there was little enough to prepare. She chose the softest material available in the Australian bush, the papery soft layers of the tea-tree bark, and with a length of it made a carry-cot or cradle for her baby. This she carried around her neck in a net in readiness for the birth.

In December 1792 Governor Phillip was preparing to leave Australia. Bennelong was persuaded to go with him, along with another native. At this time, Bennelong seemed to have acquired another wife to serve him with Barangaroo. We are not told what Barangaroo said, nor indeed whether she was angry enough to break any of his spears on this occasion.

Bennelong and his companion were the first Australians ever to visit England. Like many of the Australians who visit England today, they found the climate very trying. The lack of sunshine affected their happy natures, and the cold weather made them ill. We are told that they could not walk without the use of sticks and had lost all of their usual agility. 'Notwithstanding they are indulged in every inclination', wrote the *Sunday Observer*, 'they seem constantly dejected, and every effort to make them laugh has for many months past been ineffectual'. They were shown

A native woman with her child NATURAL HISTORY MUSEUM, LONDON

A Native Woman and Her Child.

the sights of London and taken to see the King at St James's, but they showed no pleasure in it.

One day Bennelong met an old friend he had known in Sydney, Mrs Mary-Ann Parker, the wife of the captain of the *Gorgon*. She tells us how delighted he was to see her again, and how affected he was when her little girl showed him a portrait of his old friend the Captain, now dead. He recalled their excursions in the bush together and wept. It was those 'tears of sensibility' which revealed to Mrs Parker 'the natural goodness of their hearts'. 'Soon', she wrote in her memoirs, 'the natives will no longer be considered as mere savages, and wherefore should they?'. Bennelong's companion became very thin and eventually died, but Bennelong himself was strong enough to return to Australia. He sailed with Captain Hunter in 1795, when he left to take up his duties as the second governor of the settlement. Bennelong had spent two years in England.

Back home again Bennelong began to put on airs, and assumed a haughty manner towards his old acquaintances. He treated his relations, however, 'with polished familiarity' and said that he could not allow them to go on fighting one another any longer; they must come to love one another and live peaceably together. He affected great concern over the shortcomings in their manners; and asked them whether they would mind washing themselves, and behaving in a more seemly manner, when they visited him at Government House. His own man-

Natives of Port Jackson fighting NATURAL HISTORY MUSEUM, LONDON

A Native of New South Wales surprising & wounding another whilst a sleep

ners were beyond reproach. He dressed himself with care, and at table 'conducted himself with great propriety'. Everyone said that he would now never give up the customs and comforts of civilised life.

During Bennelong's absence his wife Barangaroo had died and his young wife, Goroobarrooboollo by name, had taken a new husband. Yet how pleased she was when he gave her a very fashionable rose-coloured petticoat with a jacket and gypsy bonnet to match! He had won her back, it seemed. But a few days later she was seen naked again and Bennelong had disappeared. He had gone to fight his rival, who being a young man won both the fight and the lady—not without complaining, however, about Bennelong's new-fangled manner of fighting with fists instead of spears. Poor Bennelong was unhappy. He frequently left his clothes behind him and went bush, returning to dinner at Government House clothed again.

One day word was brought that Bennelong was too severely wounded to return to Sydney. The messenger asked for food and clothes for him. He had been wounded by his old friend Colbee when trying to carry off his wife. It is said that Colbee was very angry, and had asked him whether he had learnt that kind of conduct in England too.

From then on Bennelong was seen less and less frequently in the settlement. Sometimes reports were brought, saying that he had been wounded in a fight.

But now he no longer asked help from his white friends. He was getting old, and ugly with battle scars, and his native friends no longer trusted him. He had never settled down happily after his travels.

Although Bennelong had seen more of European life than any other Australian native, it would appear that his friendship with the white men had not really made his life happier, nor had it taught his countrymen to trust and respect the new settlers as Governor Phillip had hoped.

Excursions inland were frequently made in the first days of the settlement. The most important reason for this was the need to find fertile soil, since that around Sydney Cove was unsuitable for cultivation. Good fertile soil had been found at Rose Hill, and two settlements of emancipated convicts, with some free settlers, had been set up there. By April 1791 Broken Bay and the lower reaches of the Hawkesbury River had been mapped and named, together with the area round Richmond Hill and the Nepean River. The question remained: was the Hawkesbury and Nepean one river or two rivers? To discover the answer, a party set out from Government House at Rose Hill in 1791.

It was quite a large party consisting of the Governor, Judge Collins, Lieutenant Tench, Mr White the Surgeon, Lieutenant Dawes the Government Astronomer, three gamekeepers, two sergeants and eight privates. The natives Colbee and Balooderry, who was living at the settlement, volunteered to accompany them. They were probably encouraged to go when they heard that the journey would be a short one and saw the amount of food to be taken. Bennelong also hoped to go but on this occasion his wife was able to prevent him. Lieutenant Tench wrote up the excursion in detail, as he said, 'for those who have rolled along on turnpike roads only' (meaning those at home in England).

Everyone, with the exception of the Governor, carried his own knapsack containing food for ten days, together with a gun and a blanket. On their knapsacks they slung a cooking kettle and a hatchet, and clothed themselves 'to drag through morasses, tear through thickets, ford rivers, and scale rocks'. They started at sunrise and walked with few halts until half an hour before sunset. Even then there was no rest. For as Tench writes, 'Instead of the cheering blaze, and welcoming landlord, and long bill of fare', so well-known to English readers, 'the traveller has now to collect his fuel, to erect his wigwam, to fetch water, and to broil his morsel of salt pork'. Poor Tench found that camping in Australia was less pleasant than camping in England. The stings and bites of sandflies and mosquitoes constantly disturbed his nights. No doubt the large bull ants visited him too.

The party had set out from Rose Hill early in the morning, it being Monday, and set their course north-west by the compass, which the natives called 'naa-moro', meaning 'to see the way' in their language. Naturally this duty fell to

Lieutenant Dawes, the Government Astronomer. He counted his steps as they went, reckoning 2200 paces on good ground to the mile, and plotted their position daily. In the morning they passed over good grassy country, but later in the day they found themselves clambering up steep rocky ground for a distance of seven miles. So hard was the going that one of the party collapsed and was no longer able to carry his knapsack. At sunset, tired out by the day's march, they struck camp.

Now Phillip hoped that on this expedition the natives would demonstrate how they lived in their natural state in the bush. The natives, it seems, were equally curious to see how the white men managed in such a situation. At any rate, instead of fending for themselves they sat back, refusing to help while the others cut the wood and carried the water. The meal once ready, they came up eager and hungry to share it. After dinner, when Tench and his companions found themselves so cruelly tormented by innumerable insects that they could not sleep though completely exhausted, the natives simply rolled over by the fire and went to sleep. As Phillip and his party sat talking round the fire, the voices of strange natives were heard in the darkness of the night. Immediately Colbee and Balooderry awoke and called to them. Soon the night was filled with noise; the natives around the fire were shouting and those in the darkness were shouting back to them. At last a man appeared carrying a burning torch. At first he seemed afraid, but Colbee went out to meet him and spoke to him, which seemed to give him confidence, for he

allowed Colbee to lead him by the hand to the fire. Here he was introduced to every man in the party by name. Colbee told him that the white men lived by the coast and were travelling inland, and that they were good people.

The next morning an early start was made at 6.30 to reach the river. Phillip soon found that the natives were no use in helping him to direct the party. For they too, like the Englishmen, were outside the coastal country that they knew. So they busied themselves examining the tree-trunks for opossums' claw-marks, and left the course to Lieutenant Dawes with his compass—accepting, as it were, the white-man's superiority both in camp cooking and in plotting a course. They reached the river at a point they believed to be west of Richmond Hill. Here the river flowed 350 feet wide between high banks covered with trees. They marched down the river along the south bank for three miles until stopped by a creek too deep to ford. Pushing up the creek in search of a place to cross, the going again became difficult. The branches of fallen trees barred their way, woody creepers caught their feet, and constant stings from thick clusters of nettles frayed their tempers and set their nerves on edge. The natives, however, themselves moving over the country with ease, thought it all a great joke, especially when their masters tripped or fell. They laughed uproariously; it all seemed so funny this walking about and getting no-where. What with the rough going, and the natives' buffoonery, the Englishmen's tempers soon became pretty short. It all ended in the whitemen abusing the natives, and the natives in their language calling the whitemen indecent names.

At last next day they got to the head of the creek, and crossing it climbed to the top of a mountain nearby. This they named 'Tench's Prospect Mount', as a compliment to the Lieutenant. It was here they discovered that Richmond Hill was to the east of them, not to the west as they had expected. But the view was not encouraging: 'Nothing but trees growing on precipices', said Tench. Thoroughly tired after three arduous days, the party descended the mountain and returned to the head of the creek, where Phillip decided to camp for the night, intending next day to return to the Hawkesbury River and follow it westward to Richmond Hill. How glad they were to rest! But the natives were as fresh and lively as ever. They played 'ten thousand tricks and gambols' One moment they were dancing and singing and leaping like kangaroos; the next they were enjoying a mock fight. But most of all they enjoyed burlesquing their white friends as they fell into nettles, and slid down precarious slopes.

Nevertheless they were getting tired of the trip. They had a special way of showing their disapproval of the country. They pointed to such places saying '*wee-ree, wee-ree*', meaning 'bad'; and when mentioning a place they liked, such as Rose Hill, they said '*bud-ye-ree*', meaning 'good'. Now they began to think of all they were missing at Rose Hill. Balooderry remembered the food particularly—the potatoes, cabbages, pumpkins, turnips, fish and wine there—saying, 'Here are nothing but rocks and water'. Remembering it all, he looked up sadly and asked, 'Where's Rose Hill, where?' And to Phillip's annoyance and the irritation of the party, he kept on steadily asking, 'Where's Rose Hill, where?' It was useless for Phillip to try to explain why whitemen endured trials in pursuit of knowledge. Colbee and Balooderry thought they were pursuing game at first, and could not understand why they passed by the ducks and kangaroos. Then, on hearing that they were going to Richmond Hill, they felt sure that the Governor was searching for the special stones found nearby, from which the natives made axes. How delighted they were then next day to meet a native, Gomberee, on the river-bank, who told them that the stone quarry was a long way off! Gomberee offered the Governor two stone hatchets, and received two of his in return. Now, thought Colbee and Balooderry, surely the Governor will go back to Rose Hill.

That night they camped near the river-bank. Then Gomberee joined them around the fire, bringing with him an old man and a boy, who had followed them down the river in their canoe. The old man was a native doctor. So Colbee asked him to ease the pain in his chest caused, he said, by a spear wound long ago. The whitemen thought that he was more likely suffering from the weight of his knapsack. Then Colbee asked for a cup of water, which he gave to the old man. The doctor, taking a mouthful, spat it onto Colbee's chest, where he complained of the pain; then, putting his mouth to the part, he sucked until his breath gave out—

An emu with its egg and one of its body feathers NATURAL HISTORY MUSEUM, LONDON

all the while drawing in his stomach as though receiving the pain from his patient. The treatment was repeated three times, until the doctor, pretending to have sucked something into his mouth, threw a stone, which he had slyly picked up, into the river. Colbee felt wonderfully healed now the barb from the spear had been removed. In thanks he gave the old man his own worsted nightcap and a share of his evening meal.

After breakfast next morning, Gomberee showed his agility in climbing. Indeed all natives in these parts had to be good at climbing, seeing that they lived largely on the birds and animals which they caught in the trees. Gomberee showed how a tree of twenty feet could be scaled with the aid of a stone hatchet. The first two notches he cut from the ground. They were about one inch deep, just deep enough to receive the ball of the big toe. Climbing into the notches, the weight of his body resting on his toes, he cut a third notch; and so on, as he climbed, holding the hatchet in his mouth. While cutting a notch he grasped the tree with his left arm, or if the trunk were too thick to allow this, a notch was cut on the left for the fingers. The climbing was done in less time than it would take to climb a ladder. Even the two natives of the party were filled with admiration.

Later in the day they reached another creek, which they could not cross. This they followed only to find that it had a second arm longer than the first. So at four o'clock they made camp.

Natives of Port Jackson climbing trees NATURAL HISTORY MUSEUM, LONDON

Rain now began to fall. This was more than the natives could stand. Doubtless had they known their way home, they would have made off immediately. As they did not, all they could do was to ask where Rose Hill was. Balooderry angrily told the Governor how good the houses were at Sydney, and Rose Hill, while here they had no houses, no fish and no melons. He was very fond of melons.

The next morning even Phillip was satisfied to return. Actually little had been discovered by the excursion and the problem of the two rivers was still unsolved. The next month a small party set out to answer the question, but Colbee and Balooderry did not go with them. The party returned to Rose Hill just as a boat was leaving for Sydney Cove. The natives insisted upon embarking immediately, no doubt delighted to return to the home comforts of the settlement with the news of their adventures.

A native of Port Jackson with his fishing spear <small>NATURAL HISTORY MUSEUM, LONDON</small>

("Native of New South Wales ornamented after the manner
of the Country).

7 : CONVICTS' ESCAPE

*T*he sentence of transportation to Botany Bay, to most convicts, meant permanent exile from their homeland, and indeed nearly all those who were sent out never returned. A convict's sentence completed, no provision was made for a return passage home. So the more desperate and daring realised that the only quick way to freedom was to escape from the settlement. To the west the great barrier of the Blue Mountains hemmed them in. Many believed that they could reach China if only they could cross it. Some fled into the bush and perished, others were brought back by hunger. Others again made arrangements with the masters of ships about to sail to stow them away. So general did this practice become that Secretary Dundas took steps to stop it at Phillip's request. Masters of ships were forbidden to admit stowaways, and any found were to be put off at the first port of call. Failing to observe these instructions, the master would forfeit his contract.

An early view of the convict settlement at Rose Hill Museo Naval, Madrid

There was still another way open to the fearless and those who preferred to trust themselves to the mercy of the open sea, rather than to the mercy of their harsh masters. It was just possible to get a boat and slip through the Heads in the dark. And it could be done. After all, had not Captain Bligh sailed across the Pacific in an open boat. News of Bligh's feat had just reached Sydney, and had undoubtedly inspired some to take a risky chance.

In September 1790 a party of five convicts escaped from Rose Hill. They hoped to sail to Tahiti—that island paradise of sunny skies, where the ladies were all beautiful, food grew on the trees, and no one need work or worry. Their leader was John Tarwood, 'a daring, desperate character', according to Collins. With him were George Lee, George Connoway, John Watson and Joseph Suttor. They had all arrived at the settlement only three months before with the Second Fleet. Joseph Suttor had already made one attempt to escape, by stowing away in the hold of the *Neptune*. Somehow or other they managed to collect provisions enough to last them a week—a difficult feat in itself when the ration was so small; but they were determined men.

First they stole a punt moored at the Rose Hill wharf. Into it they stowed their clothes, bed-clothes, some iron pots and other cooking utensils, along with fishing tackle and knives. Then, under cover of darkness, they made their way down the river, past Sydney Cove and up the harbour to the lookout post on the South Head.

Here they exchanged their punt for a small boat with a sail, and escaped through the Heads in a northerly direction. They made good progress before the alarm was given. An officer in a boat was sent to make a search of the harbour; but finding no trace of them, it was concluded that the party had made for the open sea, and would certainly be wrecked.

But they were not wrecked. Sailing up the coast they were blown into a natural harbour, now called Port Stephens. Exhausted by the miseries they had endured, they landed and were befriended by a tribe of natives. They were treated with great kindness. One native believed one of the men to be the spirit of his dead father, and took him to the place where he had burnt the body. The convicts were not expected to hunt or to fight, but were waited upon as honoured guests. The convicts, who learned the native language, maintained that the natives regarded them as spirits of their ancestors who had died in battle, returning to their own people from out of the sea.

Later the men were given native names and took native women for their wives. To some children were born. Yet life was irksome. The native diet did not agree with them. They were reduced to eating not only fish, kangaroo and dingo meat, but even fern roots, with a dead whale sometimes as a special luxury. Their abdomens swelled from eating these strange foods, and they became ill. Joseph Suttor died. They slept in caves, or under the inadequate shelter of slender mia-

mias. In cold weather they shivered naked round a native fire. Here was no Tahiti of the sailors' dreams, though beautiful Venus shells were to be found on the beach and parrots of brilliant plumage screeched in the trees.

Years passed and then one day in August 1795, HMS *Providence*, under the command of Captain Broughton, was driven for shelter into Port Stephens. Three of the convicts came down to the ship and begged to be taken on board. For five years they had live as Australian natives, now they were anxious to return to the harsh discipline of the convict system, preferring it to the free life of the noble savage. They were miserable to see: naked and dirty, their skins dried by the smoke of many native fires. They could hardly be called 'white men' at all. John Tarwood, the leader of the party, no doubt fearing punishment, at first refused to come to the ship. So preparations were made to leave him a few things to make his life among the natives more comfortable. But being assured that he would be well treated, he was ready enough to join the others.

They were fortunate to return to Port Jackson at this time. Captain Broughton had already told them that Captain Hunter would arrive very shortly to become the second governor of the settlement. Colonel Paterson was making preparations for his departure. Within two weeks of the convicts' arrival from Port Stephens, Captain Hunter was sworn in as governor. Judge Collins states that to celebrate the occasion 'all prisoners in confinement were pardoned and liberated'. Among those so pardoned were probably the men from Port Stephens. It would be interesting to learn what happened to Tarwood and his friends after their return to the settlement, and to know whether they ever yearned for their old life at Port Stephens with the natives. But the records are silent.

John Tarwood's attempt to escape had really been a failure. But six months after his party left Rose Hill, a more elaborately planned escape proved in many ways to be successful. The escape was carefully planned and organised by William Bryant, the son of a Cornish fisherman, who had been bred to the sea from his youth. Arriving with the First Fleet, he was placed in charge of the fishing expeditions, which Phillip instituted for supplementing the food supply of the settlement. As the food position became more critical, so Bryant's position became one of greater importance. For as we have seen, there was a time when food was so short that everyone was expected to fish. A hut was built for Bryant and his family, and a certain part of each day's catch allotted to him. Phillip knew that Bryant was a thief and did this to dissuade him from stealing. Nevertheless he was found hiding and selling considerable quantities of fish. As early as February 1789 he was punished for these practices, but Bryant was too valuable a man to replace so he was allowed to remain in his position, though carefully watched.

Yet no one realised that behind the pilfering of the settlement's fish lay an ambitious scheme. Bryant was organising an elaborate escape to Timor. His black market in fish had provided him with considerable sums of money, which he used to buy articles and provisions for the intended voyage. These he hid under the floorboards of his hut. The Master of the Dutch *Waaksamheyd*, then in port, was also of invaluable help. From him Bryant bought a quadrant and a compass, one hundred pounds of rice and forty pounds of pork. The Dutchman also supplied a chart and information concerning the route to Timor. Bryant then bought ten hundred-weight of flour from a baker, and as many extra rations as possible. In addition he took some of the fishing tackle belonging to the settlement, some muskets and ten gallons of water.

Finally Bryant chose a crew of eleven: consisting of his wife Mary, their two young children (one three years old and one a babe in arms), together with seven male convicts, who were carefully selected. Among them were a competent navigator and a trained carpenter. Bryant himself, of course, knew how to manage a boat. It is interesting to know why some of them were transported. Bryant himself had been sentenced to seven years for smuggling, and had already completed his sentence in the colony. Mary was transported for seven years for stealing a cloak. John Butcher, aged fifty, was sent out for stealing three pigs. James Martin, aged thirty-two, was sentenced to seven years transportation for stealing about twenty pounds of old iron and lead. Nathaniel Lilly, aged thirty-nine, stole a watch,

Two convicts of New Holland

two spoons and a fishing net, being sentenced to transportation for seven years. William Allen, aged fifty-five, was sent out for life for stealing some handkerchiefs.

Although Bryant was carefully watched, and in February 1791 was actually overheard plotting his escape with his friends in his hut, yet he was able to get safely away a month later. No doubt like Tarwood and his friends, they escaped through the Heads in the night. It was probably a hurried departure. Grains of rice were found leading from the hut to the water; a saw was also found which they had dropped in their haste. One of the party, James Cox, a cabinet-maker by trade, left a note for his sweetheart. The note told her to behave herself and that she could have all of his possessions.

By the time their flight was discovered the Government cutter, which Bryant had stolen for his adventure, was well out to sea. Being the settlement's chief fishing boat, it had always been kept in perfect repair. No doubt this was one of the chief reasons for the success of the arduous voyage they now undertook. It seems that the party made their way by daily stages up the coast, putting into havens for water and to rest at night. They found the natives so hostile at most places that they had to post a watch at night, sleeping by turns. For the first five weeks it rained. At latitude 30 they found an excellent harbour, and put in to repair and grease the seams of the boat with tallow. But they were attacked by natives and had to remove themselves to a small island to get their work done. Two hundred miles further up the coast they were driven from the mainland among some islands, where they captured some turtles. These they dried in the sun and stored to replenish their food supply. Then further north still, when sailing closer to the mainland, the heavy surf swamping the boat drove them on to the shore, where they were lucky to escape with their lives. After passing through the Endeavour Straits, and past the Gulf of Carpentaria, they were chased by natives in a large canoe, the first of its kind they had seen, fitted with sails and carrying about thirty men.

Then, after a voyage of ten weeks and one day, they reached Kupang in Dutch Timor on 5 June 1791. They were well received by the Governor, to whom they told their tales of hardship, pretending to have been wrecked when travelling from Port Jackson to India. The Governor believed them and treated them with great attention. As British subjects in distress they were entitled to entertainment at the British Government's expense, and all their needs were immediately satisfied. The irony of the situation must have given the convicts some amusement, having for some years been half-starved at Port Jackson by courtesy of the British Government. But their freedom was only of short duration. One of the convicts, after drinking too much, betrayed their secret, telling the true story of their escape. They were immediately imprisoned and later handed over to Captain Edwards of the *Pandora*, who had irons clapped on them. Captain Edwards had been sent by the British Government to search for the mutineers of the *Bounty*. Returning from

Tahiti, he had struck a reef in the Endeavour Straits and had suffered shipwreck. So like the Bryants, he had himself reached Timor in a small boat. He took the escaped convicts with him to the Cape by way of Batavia, where in March 1792 they joined Captain Parker's ship, the *Gorgon*, on her way home from Port Jackson. But the party that embarked was smaller than the party that had escaped from Port Jackson. It consisted now only of Mary Bryant, her baby and six convicts. Bryant himself and his other child, together with three of the other men, had died on the voyage.

One of the passengers also travelling home to England on board the *Gorgon* was Lieutenant Tench. It was Tench who questioned the convicts and wrote a brief account of their adventures in his journal. How surprised he was to find that he had travelled out to Australia with Mary Bryant and one of the male convicts. 'They had been both of them always distinguished for good behaviour', he observes. He tells how the little party was looked upon with pity and admiration for 'the heroic struggle for liberty that they had endured'. For bereaved Mary there was still more suffering to endure. During the voyage her baby girl, now a year old, also died and was buried at sea. Perhaps Mary then wondered whether it would not have been kinder to have left her two small children behind to be cared for by the colonists. Less devoted parents would not have considered taking children on such a hazard-ous adventure, but Mary loved her children too much to leave them. The same compassion was expressed when they arrived in London and their story became known. It was generally felt that they had suffered enough. Instead of being returned to Port Jackson, or suffering death—which was the legal punishment for escaping from transportation—the Court ordered that they should complete their original sentences in Newgate, and be discharged by 'due course of the law'. A newspaper of the time comments that to the convicts Newgate was a paradise by comparison with their sufferings on the voyage to Timor. They had also found an influential friend in James Boswell.

Boswell was now nearing the end of his life. He was experiencing the literary triumph following his *Life of Johnson*, which had been published the year before. As a lawyer he concerned himself especially with poor criminals, whom no one wished to defend. When therefore he read of the arrival of the convicts from Botany Bay, Boswell hurried to Newgate to meet them. He met Mary Bryant. Now a widow and childless though only twenty-seven years old, she must have moved to pity hearts harder than James Boswell's. He met also John Butcher, Nathaniel Lilly, James Martin and William Allen and promised to take up their cause. Through his efforts in May 1793, nearly a year later, Mary received a free pardon and left Newgate in a gentleman's carriage. For Boswell still held himself responsible for her after her release. He found Mary lodgings, paid her board and gave her money for her expenses. In London she met her sister Dolly. Boswell went round to see them and greatly approved of Dolly, finding her 'of such tenderness of heart that she yet cried and held her sister's hand'. Dolly approved of him too, for he writes: 'She expressed herself very gratefully to me and said if she got the money as was said, she would give me a thousand pounds. Poor girl, her behaviour pleased me very much'.

After this meeting it was decided that Mary should return home to Fowey in Cornwall to see her father. Boswell arranged her passage by boat and fetched her in his coach. At the wharf they kept themselves warm while waiting to go on board. Boswell describes the scene thus:

I sat with her almost two hours, first in the kitchen and then in the bar of the Publick House at the wharf, and had a bowl of punch, the landlord and the Captain of the vessel having taken a glass with us at last. She said her spirits were low; she was sorry to leave me; she was sure her relations would not treat her well . . . I saw her fairly into her cabin and bid adieu to her with sincere good will.

Mary does not appear in Boswell's journal again, but he sent her £10 per annum through a local clergyman on the understanding that she behaved herself. She had given him a small gift also before she left, inscribed by Boswell on the now yellowing envelope as 'Leaves from Botany Bay used as tea'. These browned and withered leaves were later found among Boswell's papers, a piquant reminder of Mary Bryant and her sufferings.

Boswell continued to interest himself in the release of the other four convicts. A month after Mary's departure he was most pleasantly surprised to find them waiting at his front door when he returned home. They had come to thank him for their liberty.

All but John Butcher are now lost sight of. He seemed to have formed a liking for Port Jackson. Knowing something about agriculture and having, as he rather boastfully wrote to Secretary Dundas, 'a capacity of bringing indifferent lands to perfection', he wished to try his luck as a free settler at Port Jackson. Shortly after his release Butcher joined the New South Wales Army Corps and in 1795 was granted land at Petersham Hill. The escaped convict had come back a free man. Did he sometimes look sympathetically at the convicts working in their chains, and think of Mary back home in Cornwall, and of his other friends who had made the three thousand-mile voyage with him to freedom in an open boat?

The settlers soon noticed how strictly honest among themselves the natives were. As they respected one another's possessions, they frequently left their spears, canoes and fishing tackle on the rocks and beaches, knowing they would find them when they returned.

Taking advantage of this, many of the convicts collected stray articles found lying on the beaches to sell as curiosities. There was always a demand for such things, particularly when a vessel was returning home. This increased the tension between the whitemen and the natives, and unarmed convicts were frequently speared when they strayed too far into the bush. A native who had lost his spear was satisfied to avenge himself on any whiteman; it did not matter to him which one. Yet the Government was not willing to punish the natives unless their attacks were quite unwarranted.

But when these attacks became more and more frequent, measures had to be taken to stop them. It was Balooderry who was made an example of in this matter.

In 1791 the natives had been encouraged to take any surplus of fish they might catch up to Parramatta, where they bartered it for a small quantity of bread or rice. The settlers greatly appreciated this as rations were so small, and it was hoped that with encouragement a fish market would be established.

Balooderry was one of the young men who brought in fish. He had accompanied the Governor on the excursion to the Hawkesbury River, and had been living with him for some months. He frequently absented himself to go fishing.

Now Balooderry had a new canoe, of which he was very proud. Indeed it was the first he had ever owned. He took good care to leave it hidden some little distance from the wharf when he brought in the fish. One day in June, however, as he took his fish to barter with the rest, six convicts found his canoe and wantonly broke it up. This put Balooderry in a violent rage. He made off to the Governor's hut at Parramatta, carrying his spear and throwing stick. He had painted his arms, breast, face and hair red to show his great fury. He spoke wildly, saying that he would have his revenge upon all white people in any way he chose. Phillip tried to soothe him by promising to punish the offenders if Balooderry would promise not to kill a whiteman. The convicts were easily caught, as they had been seen at work. They were brought before the Governor. Balooderry was asked to watch them punished; one, he was told, would be killed. But this did not satisfy Balooderry's need to avenge himself; he wanted to right the wrong done him with his own hands. So for three weeks he awaited his chance.

Then one day a convict straying from the settlement met a party of natives and exchanged friendly greetings. No sooner had he passed on than a spear struck him in the back, followed by another in his side. Luckily he managed to get away, and was not followed.

Phillip soon heard of the attack, and returning from Parramatta the same evening he saw a party of natives seated around their fire. He stopped to ask them what had happened. They told him that Balooderry had speared the man because his canoe had been destroyed. Then, as he had broken his promise, Phillip strictly forbade Balooderry to come to any place of settlement on punishment of death. Judge Collins remarks that those who knew Balooderry were sorry he had to be treated with such harshness, adding: 'How much greater claim to the appellation of savages had the wretches who were the cause of this, than the native who was the sufferer'. As a result, the natives were afraid to come in with their fish.

Balooderry had enjoyed his life in the settlement; he longed to regain the Governor's friendship. Frequently he sent messages by his friends to see whether Phillip was still angry with him. The answer was always yes, he was still angry, and that he would have Balooderry killed for wounding a white man. Then one day in

A portrait of Balooderry <small>NATURAL HISTORY MUSEUM, LONDON</small>

August Balooderry was seen in Sydney Cove in a canoe. Bennelong was in the garden of Government House when the alarm was given and soldiers ordered to seize Balooderry. Bennelong was an old friend. Quickly he called out to Balooderry to say that the Governor was still angry and had sent soldiers out after him. On hearing this Balooderry made off to the other side of the Cove, where he was seen to brandish a spear threateningly in the direction of Government House. Some days later, he returned to the other side of the Cove again. This time he was accompanied by a party of friends, all armed. Again Phillip decided to send a detachment of soldiers to capture him. It was Nanberee, the native boy living with Surgeon White, who gave the warning this time. Slipping off his clothes so that he would not be noticed, he fled into the bush, and after warning Balooderry hid behind a tree to watch the soldiers go by. But later Nanberee showed himself to one of Phillip's servants and asked him where the Governor had gone. On being told he laughed, and said the soldiers would be too late, as Balooderry was well away already.

Now because Bennelong was Balooderry's friend, he often asked that Balooderry might be allowed to return to the settlement. Phillip had to refuse, although he knew Balooderry was a fine young fellow and had previously hoped to take him back to England with him on his return. The other natives now realised that they could safely come to the settlement, and that only Balooderry was to be punished because he attacked a whiteman.

It was not until the end of the year that Balooderry was finally brought to Phillip. Bennelong, seeing his friend very ill, had called the surgeon to him, and had got permission from the Governor to bring him to the hospital. Poor Balooderry, how afraid he was! Was the Governor still angry, and would he have him killed? But Phillip soon reassured him. Shaking him warmly by the hand, he was touched to see how ill his old friend was. He assured him that he was no longer angry, and that Balooderry should live again at Government House with him when he was well. So Balooderry was taken to hospital, overjoyed to be in favour once more, but too ill with a fever ever to recover.

GOVERNOR PHILLIP AND THE NAVAL OFFICERS in his charge made a genuine effort, within the ethical principles that prevailed in Britain during their lives, to make contact with the Aboriginal people of Australia. But, as we have seen, that could not be achieved without coercion. The brutalities were not forgotten and lingered on in the racial memory. So reconciliation between the new settlers and the first peoples of the Continent became a long-drawn-out dialogue accompanied by misunderstanding and suspicion. It is a dialogue that continues. But that some small elements of trust and hope for a better outcome could be achieved is glimpsed at times in the melancholy history of Bennelong, who more than anyone else sought to bridge the immense cultural gap between the two peoples. His efforts to do so turned him into a 'stranger' to his own people and the new settlers, and he died in 1813 a victim of alcohol. But he had pointed to a path that others would have to follow.

For convicts in New South Wales the legal and ethical codes of the time pressed even more heavily than upon the native peoples once they chose to challenge them. Few succeeded. But in the touching story of Mary Bryant and its ending with James Boswell it may be seen that humanitarian instincts could prevail over conventional values. This is true also of Governor Phillip's well-intentioned attempts to establish peaceful contact with the first people of the land that he had invaded. But here, as always, civilization exacted its heavy toll.

It was Bennelong, not Balooderry—the first known Australian Aboriginal to challenge the power of the British settlers—who ultimately gained an entry in the Australian Dictionary of Biography. Balooderry was the beginning of a forgetting.

Bennelong meeting Phillip after the Governor was wounded by Willemering NATURAL HISTORY MUSEUM, LONDON

Ban nel lang meeting the Governor by appointment after he was wounded by Wil le ma ring in September 1790

KATE CHALLIS

A Biographical Note by BERNARD SMITH

KATE CHALLIS *(1915-89) was born in London and educated at the PNEU (Parents'*
National Educational Union) School at Burgess Hill, Sussex, then at University College,
London (1935-37), where she read English, French, Latin and History. She completed a post-
graduate course in education at the Charlotte Mason College, Ambleside, in the Lake District,
in 1938. It was there that she wrote an essay 'Saint Thomas More (1478-1535)', published
in the Parents' Review, vol. 1, March 1939. Much later she was responsible for a great deal of
the research that went into the publication of 'The Architectural Character of Glebe, Sydney'
(University Co-operative Bookshop, Sydney, 1973; 2nd edition, Oxford University Press, 1989),
which we published jointly. Migrating to Australia in 1938, she taught at Mrs Eula
Broinowski's school Fairfield, Bellevue Hill, Sydney, from 1939 until 1942.
      We married in April 1941 and Kate accompanied me with our two children, Elizabeth
and John, to England in 1948 after I gained a British Council scholarship to study at the
Courtauld Institute of Art, University of London. Kate became interested in photographic

copies, obtained from the British Museum (Natural History) during the course of my research there, of works by naval artists and others who accompanied Governor Phillip to New South Wales. These included portraits of some of the first Aboriginal people that the new settlers came into contact with.

On our return to Australia in 1951, Kate decided to write a small book built around the lives of these first contacts. What she had in mind was an account that would interest pupils such as the ones she had taught at Fairfield. Unfortunately, though we made many attempts to have the manuscript published, no publisher was willing to take it on. It was before its time. So fifty years later, when reconciliation with Australia's first peoples remains a burning issue on the political agenda, 'Tales from Sydney Cove' is now at last published in the hope that it may contribute something to the reconciliation process.

A black swan, called by the natives mulgo NATURAL HISTORY MUSEUM, LONDON

Black Swan, the size of Scale of Yat an English Swan. Native name Mulga
Black Swan Latham Syn Supp. 2. p. 343.

THE DIARISTS

DAVID COLLINS: *An Account of the English Colony in New South Wales*, London, 1798.
An officer of marines who had served in America at the Battle of Bunker's Hill, Collins was appointed deputy judge advocate of New South Wales. Under Phillip, Collins was responsible for the colony's legal establishment. He shared Phillip's compassion towards the Aboriginals and generally blamed the convicts when clashes occurred. As secretary to the colony Collins was also involved with other administrative areas. His *Account* reflects this experience and in 1803 Collins was appointed lieutenant-governor of a new settlement eventually established in Van Diemen's Land (Tasmania). Collins sited the future state capital at Hobart Town, where he died after several years of harassed administration.

JOHN HUNTER: *An Historical Journal of the Transactions at Port Jackson and Norfolk Island*, London, 1793.
A naval officer with extensive experience charting harbours and coastlines, Hunter (1737-1821) had served thirty-four years at sea in peace and war when appointed second captain of the *Sirius*. His chief task was to chart the harbour and rivers around Port Jackson. In 1795 Hunter was appointed to succeed Phillip as governor. During the three years between governors the colony was ruled by the New South Wales Corps, the military detachment

that arrived with the Second Fleet to replace the marines. Their establishment of a monopoly over trade, having been granted permission to import goods, created insuperable problems for Hunter. In 1805 he was recalled by a British Government determined upon reform, although his successors too faced equal difficulties in curbing the corrupt military. Hunter eventually retired from the navy with the rank of vice-admiral.

ARTHUR PHILLIP: *The Voyage of Governor Phillip to Botany Bay*, London, 1789.
A naval captain with farming experience, who had served against the French and in the Spanish-Portuguese Wars, Phillip (1738-1814) proved an exemplary governor of New South Wales. Seeing the First Fleet safely to Botany Bay and through the ensuing famine, Phillip participated in expeditions, facilitated agriculture and exhibited humanitarian principles and an interest in reform in his dealings with convicts. He made great efforts to understand and to win the trust of the Aboriginal peoples of Port Jackson, punishing severely all who interfered with them. Departing in 1792 for medical reasons, Phillip later, as a rear-admiral of the Blue, organized coastal security throughout England during the Napoleonic Wars. Shortly before his death he was appointed Admiral of the Blue.

WATKIN TENCH: *A Narrative of the Expedition to Botany Bay*, London, 1789. *A Complete Account of the Settlement at Port Jackson*, London, 1793.
Like both Hunter and Collins, Tench (1758-1853) saw war service in America. He spent three years in New South Wales as a captain-lieutenant with the marine detachment, recording his observations on life in the new settlement in his journal. Two books resulted. They remain the most widely read of the First Fleet narratives by virtue of Tench's accom-

Surgeon White, Surveyor Harris and Mr Laing visiting Colbee near Botany Bay NATURAL HISTORY MUSEUM, LONDON

plished literary style, shrewd observations and openness to the new world around him. Following several years of service against the French, Tench was stationed at home, eventually retiring with the rank of lieutenant-general of marines.

JOHN WHITE: *Journal of a Voyage to New South Wales*, London, 1790.
A naval surgeon who had served in the tropics, White (1756?-1832) was appointed chief surgeon of the Botany Bay expedition. His performance was admirable. Few died on the voyage and within a year White had reduced the incidence of scurvy, dysentery and other maladies. A keen naturalist, he recorded his observations on native birdlife in his journal, forwarding specimens as well as drawings by Thomas Watling, his assigned convict, to London. The strain of treating the hundreds of mortally ill convicts on the Second and Third Fleets hastened White's departure from New South Wales and his subsequent career was spent on naval ships and in shipyards.

Further biographical information on the diarists may be found in the *Australian Dictionary of Biography*, vols 1 and 2, Melbourne University Press, Melbourne, 1966 and 1967.

THE ARTISTS

WILLIAM BRADLEY

First lieutenant of the *Sirius*, Bradley (1757-1833) was an experienced naval officer who assisted Hunter in his surveys of Port Jackson and Broken Bay. His independent surveys included the Parramatta River and, after the wreck of the *Sirius*, Norfolk Island. Bradley's manuscript 'A Voyage to New South Wales' (Mitchell Library, Sydney) contains both charts and water-colour views and landscapes. It also contains many observations on the Aboriginal people, in whom he was greatly interested, and Australian wildlife. Promoted captain and subsequently rear-admiral of the Blue, Bradley ended his career disgraced and in exile, convicted of petty fraud, perhaps resulting from mental disorder.

GEORGE RAPER

Joining the *Sirius* as an able seaman, Raper (1768?-97) was promoted midshipman *en route* to Botany Bay. His duties included copying charts and making views under Bradley and Hunter. Raper's views are perhaps the finest produced by a First Fleet member. A skilled artist, his numerous drawings of Port Jackson's flora and fauna were apparently drawn for his own amusement. 'They reveal a sensitive feeling for linear design and for the relationship of the image to the pictorial space, qualities in which his work far surpasses that of all the other First Fleet draughtsmen' (Bernard Smith, *The Art of the First Fleet*). Most of Raper's work is held by the British Museum (Natural History). Departing Sydney in 1791, he was subsequently promoted lieutenant, and at his death in 1797 was commander of the cutter HMS *Expedition*.

THE PORT JACKSON PAINTER

The identity of the Port Jackson Painter has not been established and in *The Art of the First Fleet* the eligibility of various candidates is reviewed. The most prolific of the First Fleet artists, his name (which may embrace the work of more than one artist) derives from the works revealing his characteristic style: the plants, animals, native people and events associated with Port Jackson. The most likely candidate is Henry Brewer, a longtime associate of Phillip's, who had accompanied Phillip as his clerk on various ships and, rated midshipman, with the First Fleet. Brewer had studied architecture and worked in the building industry before going to sea and had impressed Phillip with his all-round ability and honesty.

At Sydney Cove Brewer was appointed provost-marshall, with responsibility for maintaining civil order through the convict constabulary. Brewer is thought to have drawn up plans for the first Government House and is believed to have been the author of a large collection of drawings that Phillip prepared for examination by Sir Joseph Banks. He was granted fifty acres in the present suburb of Concord and his name lives on in Brewer Street there. He died in Sydney in 1796.

Further information concerning the illustrations can be found in Bernard Smith and Alwyne Wheeler (eds), *The Art of the First Fleet and Other Early Australian Drawings*, Oxford University Press, Melbourne, 1988.

OCEAN

MIDDLE HARBOUR

Manly
Cove

Spring
Cove

Castle
Rock

THE
SOUND

Grotto Pt

North Head

Middle Head

LANE COVE RIVER

South Head

PARRAMATTA RIVER

Breakfast
Pt

PORT JACKSON

Camp
Cove

PACIFIC

Dawes Pt

Bennelong
Pt

Bradley's Pt

Sydney
Cove

Farm
Cove

To Rose Hill

To Botany
Bay

Petersham
Hill

ARCHEOLOGY

Tales from Sydney Cove is based upon the diaries and artworks of First Fleet naval officers. They were recording traditional Aboriginal life as it was dissolving around them. The native population of Port Jackson succumbed rapidly to smallpox communicated by the Europeans. Within two years one neighbouring band of fifty was reduced to three disoriented survivors. The First Fleet diaries and artworks record a culture under pressure, fatally disrupted by external forces.

From the very beginning thefts of Aboriginal spears and fishing tackle created tension. There was a ready market for such items, particularly when a vessel was about to sail. Traditional artefacts were rapidly dispersed as Aboriginal communities disintegrated. Few are represented in Sydney's museum collections. In their absence the First Fleet diaries and the artworks, now in the collection of the Natural History Museum, London, have become the major source of information on traditional Aboriginal culture in the Sydney district.

These European records are not the only evidence of Sydney's original, indigenous residents. Excavations have been undertaken and artefacts recovered relating to different periods of occupation. Archeological evidence suggests that the Sydney region has been inhabited by Aboriginal people for at least 20,000 years. Occupation appears to have been low until around 5000 years ago, when the greater archeological visibility of the extant sites, through increased and continued use, suggests higher density of population. Changes in excavated stone tools have allowed archeologists to distinguish different phases and temporal periods of occupation. These artefacts have been recovered from open camp sites and rock shelters and from shell middens in estuarine and coastal areas. So far as Sydney Cove is concerned, two hundred years of occupation and redevelopment have obliterated almost all evidence of Aboriginal occupation. The foreshore has been altered beyond recognition and the metropolitan surface covered with concrete, its depths mined by construction and tunnelling. The freshwater Tank Stream, which attracted the colonists, now runs underground.

Recent excavations have unearthed archeological evidence sandwiched between layers of the city's foundations. In 1980 midden material was recovered from a former camp site beneath a rubble floor at the Towns Bond Store at Moore's Wharf, Miller's Point. Along with the remains of oyster, cockle, whelk and mussel shells, 392 stone artefacts were retrieved, including fabricators, flakes and cores. Fabricators were used by the Aboriginals to produce tiny flakes which may have been used as spear barbs. Longer flakes with damaged edges and small scrapers would have been used for cutting and scraping. The presence of European ceramic fragments within the soil containing this material suggests that Aboriginal use of the site continued well into the Contact period. In 1989 another smaller midden was excavated near Lilyvale Cottage in Cumberland Street, The Rocks. Rock oyster and mussel shells and snapper bones, dated to some 400 years before European settlement, link the diet of the coastal Aboriginal with today's tourist seafood platter. More recently a 1997 excavation along the Tank Stream at Angel Place yielded approximately fifty flaked stone artefacts. Their intensively worked surfaces suggest that the Aboriginals who shaped these water-worn pebbles along the Tank Stream's banks lacked access to better quality, more easily flaked raw materials.

Other archeological projects have been initiated to test the survival of material in areas undergoing redevelopment. In 1997 monitoring of site works during the construction of the Eastern Distributor yielded only a few isolated finds, while an excavation at the former Grace Bros Broadway site found no evidence for Aboriginal use of the area. Some twenty flaked-stone artefacts, emerging from excavations at the Conservatorium of Music, appeared however to derive from re-deposited topsoil rather than from the site itself.

Sources: R. J. Lampert, 'Aboriginal Life around Port Jackson, 1788-92', in B. Smith & A. Wheeler (eds), *The Art of the First Fleet*, OUP, 1988, p. 19; Godden Mackay Heritage Consultants, Angel Place Project 1997, vol. 3: Prehistory Report, Salvage Excavation of Site, prepared for AMP Asset Management, the NSW Heritage Council and the National Parks & Wildlife Service (NSW), 1998; G. Karskens, *Inside the Rocks: The Archeology of a Neighbourhood*, Hale & Iremonger, 1999.

LIST OF PLATES

The works reproduced in this book are from the collections of the Natural History Museum, London; the Mitchell Library, State Library of New South Wales, Sydney; the Museo Naval, Madrid; and the National Portrait Gallery, London.

The First Fleet art does not include any depictions of convicts. Consequently the illustrations in this book have been supplemented by two works by Spanish artists accompanying Malaspina's expedition, which visited Port Jackson in 1793. The portrait of Governor Phillip is also not the work of a First Fleet artist. It was painted in 1796, four years after Phillip had returned to England.

ACKNOWLEDGEMENTS

I must first acknowledge the magnificent way in which Valerie Haye, the publisher, has made it possible to bring this book into existence. Her interest went far beyond what may be normally expected in a publisher. For the excellent layout and design of the book I must once again thank Alison Forbes, who back in 1988 designed 'The Art of the First Fleet', the most beautiful book I have ever been involved with.

We are also deeply grateful to the Sydney Harbour Foreshore Authority for providing the financial assistance that made it possible to get our project off the ground, in particular Peter Higgins, Philippa Majors and Wayne Johnson. We also thank James Fairfax, who graciously undertook to cover the costs incurred in reproduction fees on the artworks illustrating this book.

James Wilson-Miller, Curator of Koori History and Culture at the Powerhouse Museum, read the manuscript and we were happy to hear that he was delighted with the text and felt that it would contribute its mite to the reconciliation process. I thank him for his valued support. Joan Lawrence generously provided information about certain present-day locations of eighteenth-century place names.

We are also indebted to the Natural History Museum, London, the National Portrait Gallery, London, the Museo Naval, Madrid, and the Mitchell Library, State Library of New South Wales, Sydney, for permission to publish reproductions of original artworks in their collections. Their respective staffs supplied every assistance, for which we thank them.

B. S.

INDEX